YOU CHOOSE
BOOKS

THE EPIC ADVENTURES OF ODYSSEUS

AN INTERACTIVE MYTHOLOGICAL ADVENTURE

by Blake Hoena

illustrated by Nadine Takvorian & Stefano Azzalin

Consultant: Dr. Laurel Bowman
Department of Greek and Roman Studies
University of Victoria
Victoria, BC, Canada

CAPSTONE PRESS
a capstone imprint

You Choose Books are published by Capstone Press,
1710 Roe Crest Drive, North Mankato, Minnesota 56003
www.mycapstone.com

Library of Congress Cataloging-in-Publication Data
Names: Hoena, B. A., author.
Title: Epic adventures of Odysseus : an interactive mythological adventure /
by Blake Hoena.
Description: North Mankato, Minn. : Capstone Press, 2017. | Series: You
choose books. You choose ancient Greek myths | Includes bibliographical
references and index.
Identifiers: LCCN 2015044056
ISBN 9781491481141 (library binding)
ISBN 9781491481196 (pbk.)
ISBN 9781491481233 (ebook pdf)
Subjects: LCSH: Odysseus, King of Ithaca (Mythological character) |
Plot-your-own stories.
Classification: LCC BL820.O3 H63 2017 | DDC 398.2—dc23
LC record available at http://lccn.loc.gov/2015044056

Editorial Credits
Michelle Hasselius, editor, Russell Griesmer, designer; Wanda Winch,
media researcher, Kathy McColley, production specialist

Image Credits
Dreamstime: lefpap, 104; Shutterstock: Alex Novikov, paper scroll,
Eky Studio, old stone wall, reyhan, piece of stone, Samira Dragonfly,
Baroque frame, Tymokno Galyna, Greek columns

Printed and bound in Canada.
009632F16

Table of Contents

About Your Adventure

YOU are the mighty hero Odysseus. After 10 long years fighting in the Trojan War, all you want is to return to your wife and son on the island of Ithaca. But your journey home will be dangerous. You will face mythical monsters, deadly witches, and powerful gods. Can you survive and return home?

Chapter One sets the scene. Then you choose which path to take. Follow the directions at the bottom of each page. The choices you make determine what happens next. After you finish your path, go back and read the others for more adventures.

YOU CHOOSE the path you take through this mythical adventure.

A Hero Heads Home

It's dark. You can only see faint glimmers of light through seams in the wooden planks. You raise a finger to your lips to quiet the soldiers around you. You can't risk being discovered.

May the gods be with us, you think.

You feel your hiding place shudder. You are moving slowly. The only sounds that reach your ears are the grunts of men straining and the creak of wooden wheels rolling. What feels like hours later, the movement stops.

"We're inside," someone whispers.

You hear a loud clang. *It's the city gates closing,* you think.

Turn the page.

You and your soldiers hide inside what storytellers will call the Trojan Horse. It's a large hollow statue made of wood.

For 10 years the Greek Army has battled the Trojans. But the walls around the city of Troy were built by gods. They are too strong to breech. That leaves one option—to sneak inside the city.

The idea for the Trojan Horse came to you in a dream sent by Athena herself. The goddess of wisdom has supported Greece during the Trojan War. Now she has given you the key to victory.

After the sun sets and the city has quieted, you open a trap door in the hollow statue. A soldier lets down a rope, and you quickly descend. Your men follow.

"To the gates!" you command. Your soldiers spread out.

After leaving the Trojan Horse outside Troy's gates, the rest of the Greek Army left the battlefield and hid. Your hope was that the Trojans would think the Greeks had given up and returned home. The Trojans would see the statue as a peace offering and bring it inside their walls.

That part of your plan worked. Now the Greek Army is supposed to sneak back to the battlefield after nightfall.

As you open the city gates, you see a mass of Greek soldiers ready for battle. Swords are drawn and shields are raised. Then a war cry echoes throughout the night. The Greek Army charges through the open gates.

The Trojans are taken by surprise. You hear a few clashes ring out as the Trojans try to fight back. But their city is quickly overrun. Victory is yours. After 10 long years, the war is finally over.

Turn the page.

For days soldiers shout your name. "Odysseus! Odysseus!" they call. You have become one of the greatest heroes of the Trojan War.

But your adventures are not over. You need to sail home to Ithaca. You rule the tiny island off the western coast of Greece. You left behind your wife Penelope and young son Telemachus.

Before you set sail, you thank the Greek gods for helping you defeat Troy. You offer them a share of the treasure you looted. But you have a difficult journey ahead. So you offer one of the gods a special gift in hopes of a safe trip home. You leave a token on the god's altar. Which god to you honor?

To leave a necklace made out of pearls for Poseidon, god of the sea, turn to page 13.

To leave a golden sword and shield for Athena, protector of heroes, turn to page 45.

To leave a jeweled crown for Zeus, god of the sky, turn to page 73.

CHAPTER 2

The Cyclops

You decide to honor Poseidon, god of the seas. You have to travel through Poseidon's domain to reach Ithaca, your home. You hope that the offered treasure will mean safe sailing for you and your crew.

When you set out the seas are calm, and the sky is sunny. You look forward to seeing your family soon.

But soon, dark storm clouds form overhead. Lightning dances across the sky followed by deafening thunderclaps. The wind picks up and whitecaps spread across the water.

Turn the page.

You stand at the bow and watch the rolling clouds. One of your men, Eurylochus, joins you.

"Zeus is angry," he says.

"I fear you are right," you reply.

While Poseidon is god of the seas, Zeus is the ruler of the Greek gods, as well as god of the sky. He commands the winds and the storm clouds overhead. But Zeus is an angry and jealous god, who demands respect above all others.

Turning to your crew, you shout, "Raise the sails. Tie everything down." Your sailors hurry to obey.

For the next few days, waves batter your ship. Every time the wind gusts, it feels like Zeus himself is swatting at you. The storm rages on. But just as you fear your ship will splinter apart, the winds die down and the clouds part.

Afterward you inspect your ship. Your crew looks beaten up and tired. Most of your supplies have been washed overboard. Some of the sails are torn. While all that is troubling, there is one thing that concerns you more.

Where has the storm blown us? you wonder.

You have no way of knowing. There is no land in sight. You are now lost. Still you sail on. You have no other choice.

As days turn into weeks, the sailors start to grumble. Your food supplies run low. You fear your men's anger and desperation will lead to a mutiny. So when you see an island poking out of the water, you head toward it. Green grasslands lie past the island's rocky shores. Hopefully there you will find fresh water and food.

Turn the page.

You and 12 of your sailors row a boat ashore. You hike up to the green plateau and begin your search for food. About midday, you find a cave. A well-worn path leads to the cave's entrance.

"It looks like someone lives there," one of your crew members says.

"They could have food," another says.

You walk up to the cave's entrance. The cave is dark, and you can only see the outlines of what's inside.

"Hello!" you shout, then listen. Nothing.

No one is home, you think.

To go inside, go to page 17.

To wait outside, turn to page 18.

"Light a torch," you order one of your men. He hands it to you, and then you creep into the cave. After lighting some more torches, your crew follows. They spread out all around you.

"Look at this!" one shouts. "Wheels of cheese." He holds up a large hunk of cheese for everyone to see.

"Buckets of milk!" another shouts. He lifts up a large pail. Milk sloshes down the sides.

Your sailors are hungry. One of your crew turns to you and says, "We should take what we can carry and head back to the ship."

Others nod in agreement. One adds, "There's more than enough food here. It won't be missed."

To steal the food and leave, turn to page 20.

To wait for the owner of the cave, turn to page 22.

You decide to wait outside the cave. You do not want to go inside someone's home and be mistaken for a thief.

As the sun starts to set, you hear a dull thud and feel a slight rumble in the ground.

"What was that?" one of your sailors asks.

Then there is another thud and rumble.

"An earthquake!" one shouts.

And another thud and another rumble.

There's a rhythm to the thuds, you think. Then you say aloud, "It's footsteps."

Whoever is making the footsteps must be huge. The ground shakes with every step. You fear for the safety of your men.

"Hide!" you call out.

Everyone ducks behind large, nearby rocks. As the thudding footsteps get closer, you hear the bleating of sheep. You peek around the rock you are hiding behind. You see a one-eyed giant herding a flock of giant sheep into the cave.

"It's a Cyclops," you whisper to your men.

Once inside the cave, the Cyclops rolls a large rock in front of the entrance.

Turn to page 26.

You agree. There is more than enough food here. Only a giant man could eat all of it. You have several men load up their arms with cheese. A few others grab buckets of milk.

As you walk back to your boat, your sailors are happy and laughing.

"Tonight we'll have a feast!" one shouts.

Just then a large rock falls from the sky. BOOM! The boulder crushes the man who had just spoken.

"How dare you steal from me," a voice bellows from behind you. You turn to see a one-eyed giant lifting a huge rock overhead.

"It's a Cyclops!" you yell. "Run to the boat!"

BOOM! Another rock crashes down. Another sailor is crushed.

You and your sailors run for your lives. Rocks rain down above you. Men disappear beneath them. But most of your group makes it to the beach. Your crew piles into the boat, and you urge them to row as fast as they can back to the ship. The boat lurches forward through the waves.

Back on land, you see the Cyclops step onto the beach. He holds a huge rock. He launches it into the air. You watch helplessly as it arcs toward your boat.

SPLOOSH! Wood splinters. Bones crack. Your boat is smashed. Men are flung into the sea. Many of them drown. Those who make it back to shore are snatched up by the Cyclops and eaten. You are among them.

THE END

To follow another path, turn to page 11.

To learn more about Odysseus, turn to page 105.

You decide to wait. You don't want to steal and anger whoever lives here. Instead you hope that you can trade for food. But you understand your sailors are hungry. They want to eat now.

"Gather some wood," you order. "We'll have a fire and eat while we wait."

Your crew soon has a roaring fire going. With the added light, you are able to find some bread to go along with your feast.

As you're finishing your meal, you hear THUD! THUD! THUD!

"What is that?" a sailor asks. "Footsteps?"

Whoever lives here has returned home. By the sounds of their footsteps, the cave's owner must be some sort of giant. You fear for your crew's lives.

"Hide!" you yell.

While your crew ducks into the dark corners of the cave, you quickly put out the fire. Then you find a hiding spot.

Through the cave's entrance walks a flock of *baa*-ing sheep. They are as large as horses. A one-eyed giant is right behind them.

It's a Cyclops, you think.

Once he and all of his sheep are inside, the Cyclops rolls a huge rock in front of the cave's entrance. Then he glances around the cave. He sniffs the air and snorts.

"I know you're here," he calls out. "I can smell you, so come on out."

Turn the page.

You've been discovered. You creep from your hiding spot. Your crew follows.

"Who are you, strangers?" the Cyclops asks. "And why do you eat my food?"

"I'm nobody," you say. "Just a hungry traveler. My crew and I are on our way home and were hoping to trade for some food. Who are you?"

"My name is Polyphemus," the Cyclops says with a smile. "And I'm a bit hungry too."

Suddenly he snatches up two sailors in his huge hands. They scream and kick as the Cyclops gobbles them up. Then the giant washes his meal down with a bucket of milk. Polyphemus lets out a large belch and curls up in the far corner of the cave. He is soon fast asleep.

To attack the Cyclops while he sleeps, turn to page 29.
To try to escape, turn to page 32.

You walk up to the rock blocking the cave's entrance. You lean into it, but it doesn't budge. Even if all your crew pushed, you doubt you could move the huge rock.

"There's no way in," you say.

You had hoped to trade for some food with whoever lived in the cave. But Cyclopes are not a friendly sort. They would probably make you their next meal before offering you food. So your only choice is to take what you need.

"We won't be able to get in and grab the sheep while he sleeps," you say.

"Then what will we do?" one of your sailors asks. He is afraid.

"Let's hide and wait until morning," you say. "When the Cyclops leaves, we can sneak into the cave. Maybe there's food inside."

You wake to the sound of a rock grinding against stone. You look up from your hiding spot to see the massive boulder rolling away from the entrance to the cave.

Soon *baa*-ing and bleating sheep come streaming out. Next you see the Cyclops lumber out of the cave. He leads his flock away.

Turn the page.

Once the giant is out of sight, you call to your men, "Follow me! Quick!" You light torches and head into the dark cave to explore.

"I found some cheese!" one man shouts.

"There are buckets of milk over here," another calls out.

You even find some loaves of bread. The Cyclops has enough food stored in the cave to feed your sailors for weeks.

Just then you hear the rock grinding behind you. You turn to see the boulder slam in front of the cave's entrance.

To try to move the rock and escape,
turn to page 34.

To make a weapon to attack the Cyclops,
turn to page 37.

As Polyphemus' snores echo in the cave, you call your crew. You see a mix of fear and anger in their eyes. You can't blame them. They just saw two of their crewmembers get eaten.

"We must have revenge," you whisper. "Let's slay the monster while he sleeps."

"Aye," the sailors agree. "Let's kill him."

You all draw your swords. Quietly you sneak up on the giant and surround him. Your crew raises their swords and waits for your command.

"Attack!" you cry out.

Your crew hacks at the Cyclops. The giant rolls over onto his back and roars in pain. A flailing arm sends one man crashing into a wall. Another gets stomped by a thrashing foot.

Turn the page.

Your men continue to hack and slash at the giant. As the Cyclops tries to stand, a sailor stabs him in the leg. He crashes back to the ground. He reaches for you. You slice off one of his fingers with your sword. The giant howls in pain.

Your men continue their attack. They don't stop until the Cyclops crumbles to the ground dead.

Most of your crew were either killed or hurt in the battle. Two healthy sailors go to roll the rock out of the cave's entrance.

"It won't budge," one of them calls to you.

"Maybe if we all try," you say.

You gather all the able sailors. Then you put your shoulders into the rock and push. You grunt and groan and strain and push until it feels like your muscles are about to burst.

The rock won't move. Finally you collapse to the ground, exhausted.

"It's no use," one of your crew says.

"We're trapped," another sobs.

It's true. No matter what you do, you are unable to move the massive boulder that blocks the entrance. And because of that rock, you doubt the sailors aboard your ship will ever find you.

Between the sheep and cheese, you have enough food to last for weeks. But no one comes to rescue you. Slowly you and your crew grow weaker and die of starvation.

THE END

To follow another path, turn to page 11.

To learn more about Odysseus, turn to page 105.

As Polyphemus sleeps, you gather your crew. Fear fills their eyes. They just saw two men get eaten. Any one of them could be next.

"We need to get out of here," a sailor whispers.

You walk over to the rock and lean into it. But it doesn't budge. It won't be easy for you and your crew to move.

"We must wait," you tell your crew. "If we try to move the rock, the noise could wake the Cyclops. He could kill us all."

"Then what will we do?" a crewmember asks.

"We'll have to wait until morning," you reply. "Maybe we can escape when the Cyclops leads his sheep out to graze."

You stand guard and let your sailors rest. But your men struggle to sleep.

You are still awake when Polyphemus yawns and stretches his massive arms. Then he stands. Before you can wake your men, he snatches up two of them and eats them. He washes his breakfast down with a pail of milk. Afterward he moves the rock and lets his sheep out.

Your remaining men rush to the cave's entrance. But the Cyclops rolls the rock back in place before any of them can escape.

Your men turn to you. Fear and desperation fill their eyes.

"Now what?" one of the sailors asks.

"There's only nine of us left," another says.

To try to move the rock, turn to page 34.
To make a weapon, turn to page 37.

You lean into the large rock. It doesn't budge.

"Everyone," you order. "Push with me."

Your crew joins you, but it doesn't help. The rock won't move. You point to two sailors.

"You and you, go see if you can find a log or pole that might work as a lever."

Pointing at two other sailors, you say, "You two go find some rocks we can brace the lever against. The rest of us will dig around the rock to loosen it."

Your men pull out their swords and use them as picks and shovels to chip away at the stony ground underneath the rock. The two sailors find a tree branch as thick as your thigh. It's sturdy and strong. It should work well as a lever. You set it in the hole you dug at the base of the rock. You then prop it on a pile of rocks.

"One! Two! Three, push!" you say.

Your crew pushes down on the lever with all their weight. They grunt and groan. Then suddenly, SNAP! The tree branch breaks in half.

"Now what?" one of your crew asks.

Before you can think of another plan, the rock is rolled away. The Cyclops has returned. He leads his sheep inside and rolls the rock in place.

He snatches up two sailors and eats them for dinner. After the Cyclops falls asleep, you gather your crew.

"We can't kill him," you say. "We'll be trapped."

"Then we'll have to attack when he lets his sheep out to graze," one man suggests.

You see the other men nod in agreement. You can think of no other option.

Turn the page.

Two more men become the Cyclops' breakfast the next morning. Now there are only five of you.

As Polyphemus rolls the rock away from the entrance, you draw your swords. You shout out a war cry and charge.

But you are no match for the giant. He stomps on the first man who rushes out of the cave. The next is snatched up in his meaty hand. Then large fingers reach for you. You swing your sword. It bites into the Cyclops' flesh, but the giant doesn't seem to notice. He grabs you and crushes you in his grip.

THE END

To follow another path, turn to page 11.

To learn more about Odysseus, turn to page 105.

You glance around and spot a large log. "I've got it!" you shout.

You explain your plan to your crew. You spend the day sharpening an end of the log into a point.

That night the giant snatches up two more sailors for his dinner and goes to sleep.

"Grab the log," you whisper.

It takes all of them to lift it up. Then you guide them over to the Cyclops.

"We want to blind him," you whisper, "not kill him."

You have your men aim the sharpened log at the giant's eye. On your command, they charge forward and ram the log into the giant's eye. The Cyclops sits up and screams in pain. He kicks and flails his arms and legs.

Turn the page.

The Cyclops rages on, screaming and kicking.

"I will kill you! I'll eat you all!" he yells out.

But he is unable to find you. After a long while he goes back to sleep, still grumbling threats to himself.

The next morning, Polyphemus wakes with a yawn and stretches his arms over his head. Then he feels his eye with his hand. "I will kill you all," he curses.

Polyphemus stands and blindly feels his way to the cave's entrance. Then he leans his shoulder into the rock and unblocks the entrance.

To run out of the cave, turn to page 40.

To wait for the sheep to leave the cave first, turn to page 41.

"Now!" you shout. "Run!"

You and your crew rush for the entrance. But the Cyclops hasn't moved. He hunches down with his hands to the ground. You and your men rush forward.

Suddenly the giant is a flurry of arms and legs, stomping and flailing. You urge your crew on.

You see two sailors slip past. Another gets kicked aside. Then another gets squashed.

You are the last to leave. You stop just as a giant foot slams down in front of you.

You are almost free when a hand snatches you. The giant sends you flying. Your life ends as you crash into the side of a mountain.

THE END

To follow another path, turn to page 11.

To learn more about Odysseus, turn to page 105.

The sheep bleat and baa as they start to head for the entrance. Your men look at you, waiting to make a dash for safety. But you signal them to wait. You want to see what the Cyclops does first.

As the sheep lurch forward, the Cyclops reaches out and pats the back of each one.

"Don't think you're going to escape," he calls.

Then the idea hits you. "Quick," you say to your crew. "Crawl under the sheep."

They do as you say. Since the sheep are giant, the sailors easily fit underneath them. As each sheep walks through the entrance, the Cyclops pats its back. He does not notice the sailor underneath.

"Good sheepy! Good sheepy!" Polyphemus says to his animals.

Turn the page.

Then it is your turn to escape. Once you are out of the cave, you lead several of the sheep back to your boat. Hopefully they will be enough to feed your crew until you reach home.

As you're sailing away, you see Polyphemus stumbling around on the shore. He picks up a large rock and launches it into the sea. It hits the water with a massive splash. Luckily the giant can't see, or he would take aim at your ship.

Polyphemus faces out to sea and shouts, "I hope you never reach home! May your ship sink, and your men drown!"

He continues to curse as you sail home.

THE END

To follow another path, turn to page 11.

To learn more about Odysseus, turn to page 105.

CHAPTER 3

A Witch and the Sea Monsters

You honor Athena, goddess of wisdom and protector of heroes. Athena is the goddess who gave you the idea to build the Trojan Horse. She is the reason you now sail home as a war hero. You hope she aides you on your journey home.

But she is not the one who controls the seas—that's Poseidon. And it was Poseidon who helped build the walls that protected Troy. He supported the Trojans in the war, so he is angry with you. He shows his rage by calling forth a mighty storm.

Turn the page.

The seas batter the hull of your ship. Winds tear at your sails. The storm continues for days. When it finally subsides, you and your crew are lost. You're in unfamiliar seas and have no idea where you are. Your only choice is to sail on.

You're at sea for weeks. Your supplies run low. Your sailors are hungry and grumble angrily whenever you give a command. Then you see an island ahead.

To stop and rest on the island, go to page 47.

To keep sailing, turn to page 59.

You hardly have any food or water left. Your sailors are starving. They are tired from the weeks you've been at sea. You worry that if you force them to continue any farther, they might mutiny.

"Let's see what this land has to offer," you say.

In the distance you see a column of smoke.

"It looks like a cooking fire," one of your crew, Eurylochus, says.

"I think you are right," you say. "Eurylochus, I want you to take half the crew ashore. Find the source of that smoke. With any luck we will be feasting tonight."

Eurylochus marches off with 20 sailors. While you wait for their return, you have the rest of your crew work on repairs. Sails need mending, and the storm has caused all sorts of damage to your ship.

Turn the page.

Eurylochus returns several hours later. He looks panicked, and he is alone.

"What happened?" you ask. "Where is the rest of the crew?"

"There … there was a witch," Eurylochus says.

He tells you the source of the cooking fire was coming from the home of a woman named Circe. She invited them in to feast, but Eurylochus hung back. He felt something was wrong.

After hours had passed, the men still did not come back out of the house. Eurylochus suspected the worst. Circe was a witch who had enchanted the crew.

"So I returned," Eurylochus says, "to warn you of the danger."

To go rescue your crew, go to page 49.

To sail off without your crew, turn to page 59.

You have suffered through 10 years of war with your crew. You will not leave them behind.

"Lead me to this witch's house," you say to Eurylochus.

You march along a narrow path that winds its way through the forest. At the edge of a meadow, Eurylochus stops.

"Her house is in the middle of the clearing," he says. "But I won't go any farther."

He is shaking with fear, so you don't force him. You step out from the cover of the forest and see a small cottage. The door creaks open, and a woman leans out.

"Come in," she calls to you. "I have plenty of food and drink for guests."

To go inside, turn to page 50.

To attack the witch, turn to page 52.

There is no telling what type of magic the witch has. You don't want to attack her until you know how to defeat her. But you need to go inside to find out what happened to your crew.

As you near the door to the witch's house, a man steps out from the shadows. You recognize him by the winged sandals he wears. He is the god Hermes.

"You are in danger," the god says. "But Athena has sent me to help you."

"What has happened to my men?" you ask.

"They have feasted at Circe's table and been turned into pigs," Hermes says. Then he holds out an herb with white flowers. "But here, eat this. It will protect you from her magic."

You eat the herb. It doesn't make you feel any different. But you have trusted Athena in the past, so you do not doubt her wisdom now.

After eating the herb, you rush inside the house. Inside the house, you see a large table. A huge feast is heaped upon it—roasts, bowls of vegetables, pies, and breads. Circe stands on the other side of the table.

To eat the witch's feast,
turn to page 54.

To confront the witch about your missing men,
turn to page 57.

As the witch turns to go back inside, you draw your sword and rush at her. Before you reach the steps to the porch, you hear a growl to your right. A tiger emerges from the woods, its eyes on you.

Then you hear a chorus of howls to your left. A pack of wolves steps into the clearing. Their eyes are hungry and pointed right at you.

Just then the door to the house slams shut. You run to the door and pound on it.

"Let me in! Let me in!" you scream, all the while glancing to your right and left.

The tiger and wolves are getting closer. And they have been joined by other animals—a bear, a pride of lions, and a troop of gorillas. There is no escape from their jaws as they pounce.

THE END

To follow another path, turn to page 11.

To learn more about Odysseus, turn to page 105.

You look at the feast on the table. Your stomach grumbles loudly.

"Sit and eat," the witch says with a smile. "You look famished."

Trusting that you are protected from the witch's magic, you sit down at the table. You start to pile food onto the plate in front of you.

As you eat, the witch walks around the table. Out of the corner of your eye, you see her pull something from behind her back. It's a wand. Then you feel a light tap on your shoulder. You turn to see the end of the witch's wand.

"I don't understand," she says. "My magic's not working on you."

You jump from your seat and whirl around. You grab the witch's wrist, and her wand falls to the floor.

"I have Athena to thank for that," you say, and then you draw your sword.

"Don't hurt me," Circe pleads. "I will do anything you ask."

"Then restore my men," you say.

The witch leads you out the back door. There you see a large pen full of pigs. The hogs oink excitedly when they see you.

Circe waves her wand. You watch in amazement as the pigs transform back into your men. Circe vows not to harm you or your crew as long as you don't threaten her. So you stay and feast with her. As you eat your fill, the witch tells you of the dangers that yet stand in your way as you journey home.

Turn the page.

"Do not listen to the Sirens' songs," Circe warns. "Plug your ears, or they will lure you to your death."

You and your crew listen carefully.

"To sail through the Straits of Messina," she says, "you must choose between facing the monsters Scylla or Charybdis."

After some time you decide to leave. Circe helps stock your ship full of supplies. While you haven't reached home yet, you have survived another part of your journey.

THE END

To follow another path, turn to page 11.

To learn more about Odysseus, turn to page 105.

"What have you done to my men, witch?" you say.

"I … I …" the woman stammers and backs away from you. "Just eat, and then I will take you to them."

You look down at the feast between you and Circe. Your stomach grumbles. It's been weeks since you've had a decent meal. But right now all you can think about is your missing men.

You draw your sword. The witch pulls out a wand. You knock the table out of your way and food goes flying everywhere.

With a wave of her wand, the witch disappears. You search through the house but can find no sign of her. A back door leads outside to a pigpen. You're greeted by oinks as several hogs push on the fence. It's as if they recognize you.

Turn the page.

Then you remember what Hermes had said about your men. Circe changed them to pigs. These are your men. But without the witch, you have no way of turning them back.

There is nothing you can do for them. And you don't dare take any of the witch's food. While you ate the herb Hermes provided, the rest of the sailors on your ship did not. You don't want to risk having them turn into pigs as well.

You leave the house and find Eurylochus near the edge of the clearing.

"Did you see the witch?" he asks. "Did you find the rest of our crew?"

You are upset and ignore him. You walk past Eurylochus and head back to your ship.

You are upset to have lost so many of your men. But you have lost many friends during the long Trojan War. You see no other choice but to leave the island before you lose more. Your crew grumbles about your supplies being low. But none of them want to risk meeting the witch while searching for food. So you sail off.

Then one day, one of your crew asks, "Do you hear that?" You listen.

"I hear singing," another man says. It's faint, but now you can hear it too. It sounds like women singing.

You look out from the bow of your ship. There is no land in sight. But if there are people near, that could mean food.

To sail toward the singing, turn to page 60.

To sail away from the singing, turn to page 63.

You turn your ship to follow the singing. You know your sailors are starving, and you hope that any sign of people leads to food. You stand on the bow, your eyes scanning the horizon for signs of land. Still nothing.

The singing gets louder. More and more of your crew gather at the front of the ship. As you listen, you hear words form.

"Come, young sailors. Come to me. Come, young sailors. We're so lonely."

Then you see them. Several women are sitting on a large rock that juts out of the water.

"There! There!" one sailor shouts. "We need to go there." Your men are so excited to reach the singers, you fear some of them will leap out of the ship and start swimming.

Turn the page.

When you're almost to where the women sit, a loud CRACK! erupts from below you. Men are sent flying. Some fall into the water as others slide across the deck. You know from the sound that the ship is damaged, but you don't care. You need to reach the singing women on the rock.

"Come, young sailors. Come to me. Come, young sailors. We're so lonely."

You climb onto the ship's railing and dive into the water. SPLASH! As you rise back to the surface of the water, arms reach around you. They pull you down. Then you see a flash of sharp, yellow teeth. They clamp onto you. The water muffles your screams as the Sirens drag you to the bottom of the sea.

THE END

To follow another path, turn to page 11.

To learn more about Odysseus, turn to page 105.

"We must see where the singing is coming from," one of your crew says.

"Isn't their singing beautiful?" another asks.

You see a glint of desperation in your men's eyes. They're beginning to act crazed. Obsessed.

Just then you remember a tale of beautiful sea creatures that look like women. They lure sailors to their deaths with their song.

"Plug your ears!" you shout. "Those are Sirens!"

Your men's faces turn white with fear at the mention of Sirens. Before they plug their ears, you have them tie you to the main mast.

"Don't untie me, no matter what I say," you command. "I will keep my ears unplugged, so I can tell you when we are safely away from the Sirens." Your sailors do as they are told.

Turn the page.

As your ship sails past the Sirens, their song grows louder. You fall under its spell. You lose all control and beg your men to untie you. You strain with all your might to break free of the mast. But the ropes are too tight, and they won't budge. Soon your ship is away from the danger, and the deadly song fades into the distance.

A few days later, you sail into a narrow strait. On one side is a smooth cliff. High up on the cliff face is a large cave. It looks like the lair of some sort of monster. On the other side of the strait, you see rough seas. A whirlpool swirls about and drags everything to the bottom of the sea.

As you stand on the bow looking at the scene before you, one of your crew approaches you.

"I know of this place," he says. "We're sailing through the Strait of Messina."

"What of those cliffs up there?" you ask.

"That's where Scylla dwells," he says. "She has six doglike heads that will snatch up passing sailors."

"And what about over there?" you nod toward the whirlpool.

"That's where Charybdis lives," he says. "He's a monster that lives at the bottom of the sea."

To face Scylla, turn to page 66.

To face Charybdis, turn to page 69.

"Steer near the cliff," you tell your crew.

Facing Scylla seems less dangerous than Charybdis. Scylla may try to snatch up a few of your men, but Charybdis could suck your whole ship down to the bottom of the sea.

As you get closer, you warn your men, "Keep an eye on that cave above."

You don't see anything yet, but it is best to be prepared. Several sailors keep a look out. They have their swords drawn and shields ready. The rest of your crew pull at the oars.

"Put your backs into it," you command, and the ship lurches forward.

Then one of your crew shouts, "Look!" He's pointing at the cave. You see a shadow stirring within.

Turn the page.

"Be on guard!" you shout back.

The attack is so quick and so sudden, you hardly have time to react. Six doglike heads attached to long snakelike necks dart out of the cave. Each snaps up a man, kicking and screaming, and pulls him to his death.

"Row! Row!" you shout to the surviving sailors. "Before Scylla attacks again."

Once past the cliff, your crew relaxes. You survived—again. But you are still a long way from home. You unfurl your sails. You hope the gods are kind and fill them with wind.

THE END

To follow another path, turn to page 11.
To learn more about Odysseus, turn to page 105.

There is no way for you to defend your crew from a monster like Scylla. So instead of risking your sailors in her jaws, you decide to take your chances with Charybdis.

You sail your ship toward Charybdis' whirlpool and away from Scylla's cliff. Looking back you see deadly shadows moving within the cave above.

"Row! Row!" you shout from the stern of your ship.

You don't want to risk an attack from Scylla, but you also don't want to get too close to Charybdis. Waves beat on the ship's hull. Swirling waters start to pull it forward. You try to steer your ship along the outskirts of the whirlpool. But it proves too strong.

Turn the page.

"Row! Row!" you yell.

No matter how hard your men tug on the oars, their strength is no match for the whirlpool's pull. It spins your ship around until you are dizzy. Then it draws your ship down into the center of the whirlpool. At the bottom of the ocean waits Charybdis, ready to feast on you and your men.

THE END

To follow another path, turn to page 11.

To learn more about Odysseus, turn to page 105.

Chapter 4

The Suitors

The winds are kind, thanks to Zeus. But it is a long journey home, and eventually your supplies run low. Then one day you spot an island. You see green fields with herds of large, grazing cattle roaming through them.

"We should set ashore and capture some of those cattle," says Eurylochus, one of your men.

"That might not be wise," you reply. "I've heard of this land. It's called Thrinacia. Those cattle are sacred to the sun god Helios."

"But the men are hungry," Eurylochus says. "They haven't had a decent meal in weeks."

Turn the page.

You turn from the bow and look out over your ship. Most of the sailors have stopped whatever tasks they were working on. Some gaze toward the island while others stare at you, waiting for your reply.

"If we honor Helios," Eurylochus says, "surely he won't mind that we take a few of his cattle."

If you say yes, you may anger a god. But if you say no, you will risk mutiny and losing your ship.

"If you do this," you say, "I will take no part."

Eurylochus nods and goes to tell your men. That night they have a feast on shore. You stay aboard your ship.

The next day, Helios has his revenge. The god of the sun sends a white fiery bolt of lightning at your ship. It bursts into flames. You and your crew leap into the sea.

You watch horrified as sailors drown. But there's nothing you can do for them. You are fighting to keep yourself alive. You struggle against the waves until exhaustion takes over.

The next day you find yourself alone, washed up on an island. Days turn into months and then years until you are able to build a raft and leave.

Eventually your raft sinks, and you wash up on the shores of Scheria. The king there provides you with a ship so that you finally reach Ithaca. Now that you are home, who do you go see first?

To go see Penelope and Telemachus, turn to page 76.

To visit your trusted servant Eumaeus, turn to page 85.

It has been too long since you have seen your wife and son. So you head to your home.

As you walk you notice people watch you in fear. No one recognizes you. You just hope that Penelope and Telemachus remember you.

As you approach your home, you notice something odd. The grounds have not been tended. Your animal pens are nearly empty. And strangers, men you have never seen before, lounge about. They eat your food, drink your wine, and act as if they own the place.

You head for the house, but a group of men stand to block your path.

"What are you doing here?" one asks.

To tell the men who you are, go to page 77.

To keep your identity a secret, turn to page 79.

"This is my home," you say. "I am Odysseus, returning hero of the Trojan War."

The men take a step back and look you over. A moment later, they all burst into laugher.

"So you are the mighty Odysseus?" one laughs.

"Oh, great lord," another says, pretending to bow.

"You don't believe me?" you ask, stunned. "Then out of my way!" you shout.

You try to brush by them, but they block your way. And now more men are gathering around you, drawn to the commotion.

It is then that you realize the danger you are in. You are surrounded. While many of the men openly laugh, you can see the hate in their eyes. These men want you dead.

Turn the page.

"I must go," you say, turning to walk away.

Your path is blocked. The men in your way are not laughing—their swords are drawn.

"I don't believe you are Odysseus," one of the men says. "But I don't want to give Penelope any hope that he may still be alive."

Then they attack. You draw your sword, but you are no match for their numbers. Even though you are battle-hardened from 10 years of fighting in the Trojan War, the odds are against you. You are quickly overwhelmed and killed.

THE END

To follow another path, turn to page 11.

To learn more about Odysseus, turn to page 105.

Looking around, you see many more men sitting near the front of your house. They stare in your direction. While they talk and laugh with each other, you see something in their eyes that worries you. It is a mixture of greed and hate. You have a suspicion that if these men knew who you were, they would attack you.

"I'm sorry, sirs," you say. "I don't mean to bother you."

"Then why are you here?" one asks.

"We don't take kindly to freeloaders," another warns.

You think fast and come up with a reason why you are there. "I bring a message for Telemachus," you say.

Turn the page.

"A message for Telemachus?" one of the men asks. "Ah, then you will want to talk to Antinous."

The man leads you over to a group of men who look as if they are preparing for a fight. They carry shields and wear light armor.

"Antinous," the man says to the leader of the group. "He has a message for Telemachus."

"Odysseus' brat is down by the docks, returning from a voyage," Antinous says. "I am off to go find him. I can pass along this message."

That's when you realize why the men are arming themselves. They're not just going to find your son. They plan to kill him.

"Can I join you?" you ask. "I don't care much for that brat either, but I need to tell him the message in person."

Antinous laughs. "Come with us," he says.

You, Antinous, and a handful of men head toward the docks.

"I heard young Telemachus has returned from visiting Pylos," Antinous says. "That brat was hoping to hear news of his father."

You slowly weave your way through the throngs of people at the docks.

"There he is!" one man says.

You look to the man they're pointing to. He doesn't look familiar. Telemachus was a child when you left. Yet you can see some of his mother in his features, like the color of his eyes and the tilt of his nose.

Turn the page.

"Let's end this quickly," Antinous says, drawing his sword.

The rest of the men follow his lead. One of them hands you a sword. Then they descend on Telemachus.

"Antinous, what are you doing here?" your son asks. But Telemachus must know what is about to happen. He has his hand on the hilt of his sword.

Before anyone can act, you attack. In two swift blows, you strike down two of Antinous' men.

"What are you …" Antinous starts to scream, but your son leaps into battle and cuts him off.

You are impressed by how bravely he fights. The two of you quickly put an end to the battle, even though you are outnumbered.

Turn the page.

"Who are you?" Telemachus asks.

"Son, it's me—your father, Odysseus," you say.

"They said you were dead," he says as he gives you a big hug. "I nearly believed them."

"I've faced death many times," you say. "But the gods finally saw to it that I returned home."

"We must go talk to Eumaeus," Telemachus says. "He'll help us get you to see Mother."

Eumaeus is an old and trusted servant. He is just as shocked as your son was to see you alive. All night the three of you plan how to get you inside your home to see Penelope. You can't let the suitors know you are here. So you will need to enter your house in disguise.

To go as a suitor, turn to page 92.

To go as a beggar, turn to page 95.

You have been away from home for many years. You worry that your family won't recognize you. And will your people even accept you as the island's ruler? You go to see your trusted servant Eumaeus. He has known you longer than anyone.

Eumaeus lives in a hut out in one of the fields. You knock on his door. An elderly man answers. You hardly recognize him after all these years. But you can tell by the sparkle in his eyes that he knows who you are.

"Come in. Come in," he says, ushering you into his humble home. He leads you over to a rickety table with two chairs.

"Odysseus, after all these years," he says, excitedly. "I can't believe you have returned. Ithaca has sorely missed you."

Turn the page.

Eumaeus tells you what has happened at home. Men from all over the island plague your house. They are drinking your wine, eating your food, and vying for the right to marry your wife. They spread tales saying that you are dead and never returning home.

As you're talking a young man walks in. He sees you and instinctively draws his sword.

To protect yourself, go to page 87.

To flee, turn to page 89.

Eumaeus told you that your island has become a dangerous place for you and your family. The young man who burst into Eumaeus' house looks like one of the suitors your old friend has warned you about.

You draw your sword and attack. CLANG! Your swords clash again and again.

Your opponent is no match for your skill. You knock his sword from his hand. Then you lunge, sinking your sword deep into his belly.

As the young man crumples to the ground, you hear Eumaeus shouting.

"No! No!" he cries. "Odysseus, stop!"

You turn to your old friend and see tears streaking down his face. "What is it?" you ask. "What's wrong?"

Turn the page.

He points to the man on the ground. "That is your son!" Eumaeus cries. "That is Telemachus."

"No!" you cry. You cradle your son in your arms. But there is nothing you can do. He is dead.

"What will you do now?" Eumaeus asks.

"I will do what Hercules did after accidently killing his family," you say. "I will go to the Oracle of Delphi to seek the gods' forgiveness."

"It took years for Hercules to win their forgiveness," Eumaeus says. "You may never return from such a quest."

"Then so be it," you say, turning from your friend and walking out of his home. "For I fear I will never be welcome in Ithaca again."

THE END

To follow another path, turn to page 11.

To learn more about Odysseus, turn to page 105.

You kick the table in the young man's way. Then you rush for the back door and fling it open. As you're about to dart through it, you feel a hand grip your shoulder. You turn to see Eumaeus laughing.

"Where are you going in such a rush?" Eumaeus asks. "I thought after all these years, you'd want to see the man your son has grown into."

You close the door and step back inside the house.

"Telemachus?" you whisper to the young man. "Is it really you?"

"Father?" your son whispers back. "I never thought I'd see you again." The next thing you know, your son is in your arms.

Turn the page.

"You've picked a good time to return, Father," Telemachus says.

"Eumaeus was telling me about the suitors and how they have ravaged our home," you say.

"It's gotten worse," Telemachus says. "I was coming to tell Eumaeus that the suitors have decided Mother must choose a husband tonight."

"Then we must act!" you say.

The three of you make a plan. Telemachus and Eumaeus will go to the house before you and delay Penelope. You will disguise yourself and go to the house just before nightfall.

"If our plan is to work," Eumaeus says, "no one must know you have returned."

To disguise yourself as a suitor, turn to page 92.

To disguise yourself as a beggar, turn to page 95.

Telemachus goes out and gets clothes worthy of one of the suitors. Then he and Eumaeus depart.

You wait. The hours go by slowly with nothing to do. You worry about what will happen once the suitors see that you have returned. What will Penelope say after so many years?

You leave when you see the sun starting to dip below the roofs of the nearby houses. At your house, you are surprised by how rundown everything looks. The gardens haven't been tended. The animal pens are empty. And men you have never seen before lounge around, chatting and drinking your wine. But when they see you walking toward the house, several of them stand to greet you.

"And who might you be?" one of them asks.

"My name is Eurylochus," you lie, using the name of one of your lost crewmen. "And whom might you be?"

"Eurymachus," the man says. "What is your purpose here?"

"To seek the hand of Penelope in marriage," you say. "The same as you."

Eurymachus motions to the men gathered around him. "So do you feel that you are more worthy than the rest of us?" he asks. The men at his side laugh. But there is nervousness to it, as if they know Eurymachus' intentions aren't friendly.

Turn the page.

"That is for Penelope to decide," you say.

"Well I'm not about to welcome any more competition," Eurymachus says. He steps back and draws his sword. The other men do the same.

They attack as you draw your weapon. CLANG! The clash of steel rings out. You cut one man across the shoulder. You stab another in the belly. But there are too many to fight alone.

You feel a sword cut your thigh, and you fall to your knees, dropping your weapon. Eurymachus stands over you, sword raised.

You see Telemachus burst from the house. But he is too late. Eurymachus swings his sword. You crumple to the ground, lifeless.

THE END

To follow another path, turn to page 11.

To learn more about Odysseus, turn to page 105.

You sort through some of Eumaeus' old clothes to disguise yourself as a beggar.

Once the sun sets, you head out toward your home. People avoid you. They see your ratty clothes and dirty face, and they steer clear of you.

To your surprise, that is how things go when you reach your home too. Suitors lounge about on your property. You pass by them unnoticed.

It's not until you reach the door that anyone pays you any attention. A man stands in your way.

"We don't allow your sort in here," the man says. He is one of the suitors. Other suitors behind him turn toward you. But you don't see any sign of Telemachus or Eumaeus.

"Please, sir," you say. "Just a bite to eat."

Turn the page.

A man throws a scrap of food at you and says, "Here, now begone."

Just then the room goes silent and all heads turn. They watch a woman, your wife, enter from an interior door. She is with your son.

You want to go to her and tell her how much you have missed her. But Telemachus catches your eye. It is not time to act.

Then Penelope looks in your direction. She doesn't recognize you.

"The needy have always been welcome here," she says. "Let the man in and give him food."

"We will do whatever you wish," a man shouts, "as soon as you select your new husband."

Penelope sighs, defeated. Telemachus is brushed aside, as several suitors crowd around Penelope and make their demands.

You glance over at Telemachus. You see the anger in his eyes. In one corner you spot Eumaeus. He scowls at the scene before you.

"Yes!" a suitor shouts. "You must choose."

"You've kept us waiting far too long," another says.

The men are jostling for a position in front of Penelope. You can tell they are tense and jealous of each other. You fear a fight could break out at any moment.

"Quiet! Quiet!" the men shout, waiting for Penelope to speak. They all go silent as she speaks her first words.

Turn the page.

"I will choose a husband," she says. "But only under one condition."

"What is it?" a suitor asks.

Telemachus walks over to one wall of the great room. There hangs your old hunting bow. He pulls it off the wall and brings it to Penelope.

"Odysseus was a great man," she starts. "I will only marry a man that is his equal. This is his bow. The man who wishes to marry me must be able to string it."

The room erupts in shouts as men demand a chance to try.

You watch as your bow is passed from man to man. Each suitor tries to bend your bow and attach the string. Each suitor fails, unable to bend it. They grunt and groan, curse and yell.

Turn the page.

"Impossible!"

"It can't be done!"

They are starting to get unruly. Then Eumaeus catches your eye in the corner of the room. He pulls out a quiver of arrows from his robes. You know what you must do.

"Let me try," you shout over the men. The suitors turn to you.

"You don't have the right to marry Penelope," one suitor says.

Others scoff. "Let him try," one says. "If anything, we'll have a good laugh."

The great bow is handed to you. You prop one end between your legs. With one hand, you bend the bow while the other hand pulls the string. It is not easy. Your arms shake from the exertion. But you are able to string the bow.

The suitors let out gasps of disbelief. Penelope looks at you stunned.

"Can it be?" she whispers.

Before any of the suitors can react, Eumaeus tosses you the arrows. Telemachus steps to your side and draws his sword.

You release several arrows, killing a handful of suitors before anyone realizes what is happening. Then chaos erupts. Some men attack. You and Telemachus quickly strike them down. Others try to flee only to find that the doors are locked. In the confusion, Eumaeus had snuck out and barred the doors from the outside. You and Telemachus strike those men down too.

When the battle is over, only you, your wife, your son, and Eumaeus are left alive.

Turn the page.

"Odysseus, my husband. Is it really you?" Penelope sighs.

"It is, Mother," Telemachus assures her. You grasp your wife in your arms and pull her to you.

"It is I," you say. "After all these years."

Finally you have been reunited with your wife and son. Your journey is over.

THE END

To follow another path, turn to page 11.

To learn more about Odysseus, turn to page 105.

CHAPTER 5

King of Ithaca

Even after her husband strung his old bow and slayed the suitors, Penelope was unsure that Odysseus was who he claimed to be. She had not seen her husband for many years. It was just too hard to believe that Odysseus had returned. She had one final test for him.

So that Odysseus could overhear, Penelope asked a servant to move Odysseus' bed from their bedroom. She knew that only Odysseus would know this task was impossible. Odysseus had carved the bed from the stump of a huge olive tree, and it could not be moved.

Turn the page.

Upon hearing her request, Odysseus told his wife, "There is no man living, however strong and in his prime, who could move the bed from its place." With those words Penelope knew it was true. Her husband had returned home.

But the trouble was not over for Odysseus. He had slain many of the men on the island. Their families wanted revenge. Soldiers gathered and a battle soon took place.

Athena was tired of the bloodshed. She appeared before the soldiers. Many of them were so afraid upon seeing the goddess, they stopped fighting. Athena made both sides swear a truce, and there was peace once again in Ithaca.

Odysseus regained his position as ruler of Ithaca. And unlike many other mythic heroes who had tragic endings, Odysseus led a peaceful life with his faithful wife and son.

Greek Gods and Goddesses

Athena—goddess of wisdom and the protector of heroes. In many Greek myths, Athena provided heroes with help to succeed on their quests.

Helios—god of the sun. Helios drove the golden sun chariot across the sky everyday to raise the sun. Four winged horses pulled his chariot.

Hermes—messenger of the gods. Hermes flew around the world on a pair of winged sandals. He was also protector of travelers and often carried messages from the gods to human heroes.

Poseidon—god of the sea and Zeus' brother. Poseidon helped build the walls around Troy and had sided with the Trojans during the war. He hated Odysseus for helping the Greeks win. Polyphemus was one of Poseidon's sons. After Odysseus blinded Polyphemus, Poseidon tried to keep Odysseus from returning to Ithaca.

Zeus—god of the sky and ruler of the Greek gods; father of Athena. Zeus was also the father of many of the most famous Greek heroes, such as Heracles and Perseus. His weapon was a thunderbolt.

OTHER PATHS TO EXPLORE

During his 10-year journey home, Odysseus had many adventures. You just read some of the most well-known stories. These include blinding the Cyclops Polyphemus, meeting the witch Circe, navigating past the Sirens, Scylla, and Charybdis, and slaying the suitors who had overrun his home in Ithaca. But there are many other tales that were not included in this book. Here are some of Odysseus' other adventures for you to explore.

1. After leaving Troy and having his ship blown off course, Odysseus first came across the land of the Lotus Eaters. The natives there chewed on the sweet and delicious lotus flower, which caused them to forget all their worries. Why do you think Odysseus would want to taste the lotus flower? Do you think Odysseus would have still made the journey home? (Integration of Knowledge and Ideas)

2. Among the many helpful things she told Odysseus, the witch Circe also told him to go to the Underworld. In the land of the dead, our hero sought out the seer Teiresias, who warned him against eating the cattle sacred to Helios. How could Odysseus have stopped his angry and hungry men from eating some of the sun god's cattle? (Integration of Knowledge and Ideas)

3. After his ship was destroyed in a storm and all of his men drowned, Odysseus washed up on the shores of Calypso's island. Calypso was a sea nymph, who kept our hero captive for many years. Calypso even wished to marry Odysseus. What would Odysseus' life be like if he had stay with Calypso? What would happen to Penelope and Telemachus if Odysseus did not return home? (Integration of Knowledge and Ideas)

Hoena, Blake. *The Voyages of Odysseus:
A Graphic Retelling.* Ancient Myths. North Mankato,
Minn.: Capstone Press, 2015.

Jeffrey, Gary. *Odysseus and the Odyssey.*
Graphic Mythical Heroes. New York: Gareth
Stevens Pub., 2013.

McMullan, Kate. *Get Lost, Odysseus!*
Myth-O-Mania. North Mankato, Minn.:
Stone Arch Books, 2015.

INTERNET SITES

FactHound offers a safe, fun way to find Internet sites
related to this book. All of the sites on FactHound have been
researched by our staff.

Here's all you do:
Visit *www.facthound.com*
Type in this code: 9781491481141

GLOSSARY

bleat (BLEET)—the cry made by a sheep or goat

boulder (BOHL-duhr)—a large rounded rock

Cyclops (SY-klahpz)—a one-eyed giant

grassland (GRASS-land)—a large, open area of grass, often used as pasture for animals

honor (ON-ur)—to give praise or show respect; the Greeks could honor their gods by giving an item, such as a valued treasure

mutiny (MYOOT-uh-nee)—a revolt against the captain of a ship

plateau (pla-TOH)—an area of high, flat land

Siren (SYE-ruhn)—half bird, half woman creature that lured sailors to them by singing; singing Sirens caused ships to crash near their island

Trojan War (TROH-juhn WOR)—a 10-year war between the Greeks and the Trojans; the Trojan War started after a Trojan prince kidnapped Helen, the wife of a Greek king

BIBLIOGRAPHY

D'Aulaire, Ingri and Edgar Parin. *D'Aulaires' Book of Greek Myths*. New York: Delacorte Press, 1992

Homer. *The Iliad*. Project Gutenberg. http://www.gutenberg.org/ebooks/2199

Homer. *The Odyssey*. Project Gutenberg. http://gutenberg.org/ebooks/1727

Virgil. *The Aeneid*. Project Gutenberg. http://www.gutenberg.org/ebooks/22456

INDEX